SEGUES

WS
MB

SEGUES

A
CORRESPONDENCE
IN POETRY

WILLIAM
STAFFORD

MARVIN
BELL

DAVID R. GODINE, PUBLISHER
BOSTON

First published in 1983 by
David R. Godine, Publisher, Inc.
306 Dartmouth Street
Boston, Massachusetts 02116

Library of Congress Cataloging in Publication Data

Bell, Marvin.
Segues: a correspondence in poetry.

1. Epistolary poetry, American.   2. American poetry—
20th century.   I. Stafford, William Edgar, 1914–
II. Title.
PS593.E63B4   811'.54'08   81-47319
ISBN 0-87923-410-5   AACR2
ISBN 0-87923-484-9 (pbk.)
ISBN 0-87923-483-0 (deluxe)

SEGUES
was set by Maryland Linotype in Electra, a face designed by
W. A. Dwiggins (1880–1956). It was printed by The Courier
Printing Company, Inc., Littleton, New Hampshire, and bound
by New Hampshire Bindery, Inc., Concord, New Hampshire.
The paper is Warren's #66 Antique, an
entirely acid-free sheet.

Text and jacket design by Jeffrey Schaire
Calligraphy by Jack Harrison

First edition

Printed in the United States of America

Grateful acknowledgment is made
to the editors of the following periodicals
in which these poems previously appeared:

THE AMERICAN POETRY REVIEW: *Serving with Gideon; Accepting What Comes; Air Wisconsin; More than Words Can Tell; Conscious Dog; Reading at American University; Who's In Charge Here?; What to Say; Zero; Nothing Special; Then; It Still Happens Now; Crooked Water Ways; Key of C—an Interlude for Marvin;* and *The Years 1950–54.*

FIELD: *Hunger for Stories; The Part I Know; Things Not in the Story; Suppose,; Hunting What Is; Slow; Telling You Carefully; Reflexes; Serving with Gideon; A Further Response; Losers; It's; Meeting Big People; Flyswatter; The Permission of the Snow; Schooling, Then and Now; Learning, Any Time;* and *Turning on a Lamp.*

HAWAII REVIEW: *Dear Marvin,; About Our Series; Living Far Enough Away; At the Writing Conference; For an OK Writer;* and *Seeing that Things Happen.*

PEQUOD: *Things Not in the Story.*

POETRY MISCELLANY: *Hunger for Stories; Testing, Testing, Not Being Lost; Wherever You Are; Before It Burned Over; What the Czar Said to the Grass; Just Some Names;* and *"Words that Mean More than Just Sounds."*

THE RUNNER: *Slow.*

Contents

Contents

The authors would like to extend special thanks
to Steven Cramer,
who was instrumental
in bringing this book to publication.

Preface

It was at The Midnight Sun Writers' Conference in Fairbanks, the summer of '79, that we decided on SEGUES. We didn't want to give up the momentum of that serene time in Alaska, the easy interchange, the motivation for writing.

What if we tried playing annie-over with poems, **we** thought, lofting one to a partner over the miles, and then waiting to see what would come back? This book is the result of that experiment, the poems we lobbed back and forth during the next two years—twenty-two poems apiece, loosely linked, growing out of each other.

We didn't know where we were going, and we didn't care—it was just an idea, one way to maintain momentum in our writing. You don't always have someone near to give a new poem to: this way, we always had a reader, a receptive person to give a glance and maybe an opinion.

Actually, the suggestions and opinions we expected hardly ever happened. We wrote the poems and sent them off, waiting for the rebound and finding each time that what came back was a furthering of what had gone before and an invitation for the next move. We didn't hold ourselves to close connections; often we took off sideways. But always it was a little bonus, the mail was, to have a writer friend, ready, an alert reader, an active partner.

We suggest to other writers some possibilities in this kind of corresponding. No matter where you live, you can solve several little problems at once. Where do I find a reader for this new piece of writing? (Many of us are not surrounded by people who are eager to give sustained attention to our necessarily tentative efforts.) How do I maintain that feeling of living in a responsive world? (Satisfying as it is to accomplish the experiences of writing on your own, it is natural to be sociable, too, about language.)

The stray feelings and thoughts, the strange little bonuses when you push words toward each other, the easy to neglect but inwardly significant events of your life—keeping in touch is a way to welcome those happenings, to link and confirm them, there on the page, between friends.

—WILLIAM STAFFORD

Preface

[1]

SEGUES began when we agreed on it during the first Midnight Sun Writers' Conference, held in June 1979 in Fairbanks, Alaska. I went home and tried to write something about Alaska and us. Before I could finish, there was Bill's first poem, "Hunger for Stories." Since, each poem has come in some way—narrative, argumentative, emotional; or just agreeably—out of the previous poem. There have been slowdowns on my part. I went to Italy and lost my writing for five months. Bill has been always ready. He and I are different generations, from very different backgrounds, and he moved from the Midwest to the Northwest while I moved from the East to the Midwest. We make our differences in our poems. But everything there is to say about poetry is contained in the word "correspondence."

Also, it brightens the mail.

[2]

I had thought before about poems back-and-forth. There's good luck, not to say advantages, in addressing someone in particular in one's writing—the more so, perhaps, if you and the other are different in the details of your lives but neighborly in the ways of your minds.

Also, I like deadlines and assignments. My feeling has been, as has Bill's, that the writer can begin anywhere. For Bill, that has meant a continuous outpouring of great variety, but for me it has sometimes meant writing by fits and starts. The freedom to begin anywhere and to pay attention or not—the freedom that is art—confers on me from time to time involuntary silences. The encouragement to speak in turn and a text from which to begin—these, for me, are liberating.

Also, left to oneself, one often goes hard in a single direction. A series like this, however, is incremental, overlapping, with eyes front and back and chances to rest.

There are ideas and stories here, but it is the idea and story of the ongoing series that wanted for examples, and welcomes more. We ourselves have written past the covers of this book: the signal of a willingness which lies at the heart of any writing, and which must be cherished or all fall down.

—MARVIN BELL

SEGUES

Hunger for Stories

By now it's not Japan or a bell
when I touch the world at night and bring
the strange echo. It's not the little trumpeter—
secretly myself—trudging miles
through the snow and dying after he saves
the emperor on his big black horse.

It's another story—not that sure
voice telling how we came, the world
shivering again. I listen farther
out into the waves. The emperor stalks away.
I am a tree and can't move.
It's not Japan or a bell.

Then a bell sounds.
An old man comes along.
He looks into my face:
a child is wandering out into the snow;
everything is telling one big story.

The Part I Know

A bell may tell this story:
a young man—myself,
though I won't know this for years—
by the side of a cemetery road;
a man his father knew
pinches his cheek.

For twenty years,
things occur not in the story:
life with bigger skies,
stars that line up heroes.
His father cannot move to join him;
there are many little stones on his big stone.

A breeze will move a road,
and a ghost push us.
Sometimes, I look. I pinch off
a part of the story I know;
toss it to you. And other parts to
my mother, Belle, and my sister, Ruby.

Things Not in the Story

Most things are impossible. But I think
them all. Before they happen, I climb
ahead and call back—"This way!" They follow,
though sometimes awkwardly till I tell them exactly
how to move—even what to look like.

I coach them along and invent their reasons,
or why they don't have any. In the mountains
I often create shadows and echoey sounds;
but in the desert—a few high, thin
voices and bright light everywhere.

But sometimes I sleep and falter, and many things
never happen at all. In my dreams—
and somehow under my dreams too, at a level
where I don't quite exist—a great moving
carpet mutters and heaves, of things wanting to be.

I remember my mother hearing the heartbeat
under the floor, and my father saying
it's nothing—and knowing that that is the worst
of all: for the sound you hear from nothing
may never stop; it may fill the whole world.

Once when she looked I saw myself
taken back into her eye: if only
I hadn't been born, maybe all else
had come true; and I pitied her: "I'm sorry."
And I tremble still—the helper—and the source—
of her sorrow.

Suppose,

---

after years of letting things
happen, a person
decided not to let things happen
unless called. Names
would have to be changed:
your wife and mine couldn't
both keep Dorothy; your mother,
having died, could keep Ruby,
but my sister, only having
almost died, would have to change
her name—a shame,
Ruby Bell having a red sound
the color of life itself in the ward
where she works. Well,
we could make exceptions. I tried,
once, to: 650 miles
to the mountains of Mexico
before the Olympics paved it,
first day, first hour,
walking through a garden
toward my room, a street-vendor's ice
to sugar me awake, and to my right
suddenly in the shade
a friend ten years before.
I kept walking; I refused.
I didn't call. Instead, I made this other
story happen. I wonder if I
could tell it if it hadn't.
This may be a weakness:
I tend to believe.
My father's name, Saul, in Russia
was Russian; in our town, Sam.
The one other Ruby was a man.

My father's brother married my mother's
sister, both older, after
Harry and the father made the money
to bring over the family.
In Venice, their suitcase and papers
were stolen. They placed an ad;
it was all returned! Otherwise,
I'd be living in Siberia,
where things that happen otherwise
don't, but other things do.

Hunting What Is

There are days when everything waits—you run
down the street, and it's cool, and now has a light
inside it, and you are entering that light
as a part of time, by giving your look—

But things are hiding. As you run the street
angles widen ahead even as they close
behind. True, you felt close, back there,
but what opens is also true, and the street. . . .

So it all marks your life—what you pass
and almost find will define your part.
You claim, "Things are happening to me!"
And the world goes hovering on as you pant, "Mine."

Slow

I go out to find whatever comes
but the first fifteen minutes
are for trying to breathe, the next
fifteen for using both legs
without almost having to count
cadence, and the second half hour
for water, two cheeps at a bird,
and the reassurance that important chemicals
are now in the bloodstream. The first
fifteen minutes are the hardest,
anyone will tell you that, the first thirty
are the hardest, and the first hour
is the hardest hour, but in the second hour
something goes right without your knowing:
a mixture of good motions, oxygen
and a certain giving-up
that permits you not to hurry
and gives you back for every slow minute
two that are beyond you. It's the slow
who have to keep going who get to take back
the possessive note they struck
when they were strong. Weak, they find
fatigue is buoyant, they can coast, float,
and they sometimes have thoughts
too pure to be brought home
but not righter than others, despite
what you see on the talk shows
with your legs up and your toenails blacker.
Out-and-back runs, says David,
are like folding a piece of paper.
At the far end, you know what to do.
Loops are the worst, repeating what you see
as if you owned it. You look forward
to the past; the run lengthens.

I like runs that take a hill in one direction,
pass a body of water,
go down one street no one knows,
and find a breeze. Most of us save the long run
for Sunday, which is sensible
not religious. No believer, after all,
but no doubter, I do
look around, except uphill, the more so
after the first two hours
(when it gets easier).

Telling You Carefully

Part of the time I want to tell you
something so clearly you get there before
I finish. I want you to know and be sure of
more than I'm saying, be ahead of me
so far I'm clearly just dull. I could just bark
like a well trained dog. Why? You can
decide—I don't have to win anything.

Even back there at school I didn't have need
to perform well—there was something else:
back of the classroom I felt it, or it was
breathing when we looked up, afternoons.
My sister, too, watched whatever happened
on the way home, and reported it, sitting
in the kitchen eating crackers and milk.

I'd listen and say yes or no, and nobody
cared if I'd won anything, or lost:
there was a show—the world surrounding
our house; we were to go there and be good
and come back and tell. That's what we did.
Our mother thought we couldn't control
events or prevail, really, anyway.

We had a routine so calm that only
the weather counted in the news. "In the spring
we'll have a circus at school," I said.
A wind blew the curtain. I looked out over
the yard. "Our teacher in history said
they'll make mistakes again and we'll have a war."
There—you see what I mean?—you *knew*.

Reflexes

There was a powder the druggist had—
used it on my hand when I squeezed
a glass ornament at Christmas: I
picked it up, held it up and held it tighter,
three stages I can still distinguish.
Then I was holding a handful of blood.

This man's oldest daughter died
from a dormitory fire—famous at the time.
She got out, then went back.
She lay for days in the burn ward.
She had been skinned alive. No chance.
Her father, the pharmacist, understood.

Sometimes, you have to imagine the worst
to prepare: the calm fire drill at school,
or the desperate decisions that come
in the dark: which room, which child?
We fuzz it up with heroics, charades.
No one can picture the worst.

Serving with Gideon

Now I remember: in our town the druggist
prescribed Coca Cola mostly, in tapered
glasses to us, and to the elevator
man in a paper cup, so he could
drink it elsewhere because he was black.

And now I remember The Legion—gambling
in the back room, and no women but girls, old boys
who ran the town. They were generous,
to their sons or the sons of friends.
And of course I was almost one.

I remember winter light closing
its great blue fist slowly eastward
along the street, and the dark then, deep
as war, arched over a radio show
called the thirties in the great old USA.

Look down, stars—I was almost
one of the boys. My mother was folding
her handkerchief; the library seethed and sparked;
right and wrong arced; and carefully
I walked with my cup toward the elevator man.

A *Further Response*

This time I've some headlines for you:
Wind Rips Branches, Bells Find Home—
this latter old news made new
by changes the town Fathers
have made here in my town. There used to be
a hotel, the Burkley, you remember,
in the center, a kind of passage between
the Greyhound Depot behind
and the college across the street.
Hundreds of messages go under that street
now, since the jackhammer.

We found a place to live in the elevator
at the Burkley; I mean,
you have to call to mind the accordion
grille and the steering wheel
and the driver's stool and the outside
mirrors at each floor—all
to hear the help talk up and down the days.
My son rode up and down, helping.
We're looking for a place, he told them.
A few short trips, a correction or two
to floor level, and he had found one
there in the valve of the Burkley.

The tip proved out. We had a house.
Its rooms made a spoked wheel
and I moved into the turret to type out
signals like these. I was just out
of the Army, remember. In any discussion,
whoever *they* were, I was one of them.

It was the Sixties, think twice!
Never mind me, I tore that person down
that I was, and when trees broke in the wind,
I thought again of the elevator man
who held his job with one hand, and extended it.

Losers

You learn from losers. You give back their sounds
with a little twist and yielding becomes an art.
You assume the present and find your needs wherever
you are. Your oppressors are never to know they're
in a war. "Yes" is the sound of breath at its easiest.

I found a place by a lake one time where I camped
for a week. I never spoke, even a whisper.
It's cold up there, and hot, and when the wind
goes by it shrieks. At the end it was goodby
with only a wave. I was a careful loser
headed north, carrying all I would need.

If the world had asked me to stay I would have stayed.

It's

---

taken me a month to reply to your letter.
Couldn't figure out why.
I liked the word "lake" right away.
I had ideas about "Yes," and
fortune-telling. It even appeared to me
that "No" would not be an answer,
but what occurs while you
are waiting for an answer, maybe
even fearing an answer.

But then "losers," "Losers!"
"Losers" and "Yes" and the "lake."
I know drowned people,
I'm Coastal as you know, have no dry
illusions about men in water.
That's not it either:
my experiences, people I know, none
of that is it. It's
a picture I saw.

Before these things were more than
known about, when few men
and fewer women had looked at such things,
I was Army-indoctrinated,
and looked at combat footage
that led the camera from landing ship
to inland camp in Nazi Germany.
You can guess what "camps" these were.
Those piled bodies of the losers

taught me nothing. Oh, I was more than
just moved; I'd have killed.

Meeting Big People

We would sit down, after a visitor had
gone (reassured by lavish agreeable responses
and strokings), and my mother would not hide from
me her great treasure of saved-up reflection
on the oddity, poverty, blundering of the
just-pampered person who had been soothed. I
learned how kind you have to be so as not to
let others know their truly desperate situation
("Don't let them know!")—they are *other*.

Big people huff up like a cat, fierce or
scared. You hurry over to say, "You are big,
huffed-up, fierce." You don't say "scared"—
you want to meet them where they are. Your
expression studies theirs and becomes whatever
they need. When you leave them you often say, "Scared."

Once, away from the sound of the highway, we walked into
silent Wyoming, a hawk riding a thermal, one
smooth hill drawing our world into the sky.
Side by side we angled the hill, treading tough short
grass, now and then choosing which way to
avoid an arroyo. Mostly the spacious landscape
allowed straight, air-free walking. She told me:

Let's consider describing geniuses the way we describe
popular figures: How tall was Einstein? Pascal? Napoleon?
Eve Curie? Thomas Aquinas? Dante? Mother Mary? Mo-
How impressive was Plato? Confucius? Aristotle?   [hammed?
Gandhi? Descartes? Shakespeare? Keats? The Brontës?

She thought the aggressive were losers. They had to use
methods only the desperate would use. Their lives were
ruinous. Without even knowing it, they forfeited
the game before they got started. She studied them and
shook her head. But to tell them would hurt them without
curing their disability. To an extreme degree they had
that almost universal burden of being other.

How can you keep others from feeling the abrupt
fact that they are—don't say it to them—other?
You listen carefully, and never allow the hail
of their multiple little blunders—or the vast
arc of their wild misunderstandings—to register
in your unswerving, considerate gaze.

The one who appears hurt, I learned, could be
the one who is withholding hurt from the others;
and for those of us rich in this wide, mild
gaze, we'd be worse than the others if like them.
This was her way—to suffer, lose wide-eyed, and
practice the ultimate put-down of her secret *noblesse oblige.*

Flyswatter

Remember the great permission the blizzard gave?
School was closed. We could take a day off
from trying to improve ourselves. Trees that fell
fell into places we were watching and we saw
a farther snow hesitating overhead. And we let go.

For as long as school was out, we were not
a coach's courage, teacher's pet or hero
to a schoolyard ready to fight to be what others
required. We were not the losers, either.
In the cold classrooms, the blackboards and the chalk.

I knew the odd man who had volunteered
to mind the library house two nights a week.
I stepped into deep snow to make it there.
Keeping the books he mentioned past due
cost me money. Sometimes, he undercharged me.

Odd people everywhere underwrote my education
and I remembered the odd: Gandhi on the railroad
tracks while the British threw pots of urine,
Descartes with his head bowed, Shakespeare
sonneteering a shadowy love, Keats drowning,

and Einstein said to have failed a math test!
Kids, kids, what does kids know? Can I say?
They know joy without virtue. They are told
and told they do, but they don't: they don't sin.
I was only afraid and wanted to be like others.

The Permission of the Snow

The perfect snow that told your face which way
was north, and how the sky was where you'd go
if you were good—we knew those promises.
I'll try, before I give that world back,
to straighten it:—
                    You teachers of mine, you had
us wrong: we were sorry for you. Miss Devoe
in love with what's his name the light-foot coach
with a whistle around his neck, and Mr. Wicker
in shop, that no one loved—even then I knew
what the world was like. When we marched in
to Sousa's music, right at the turn
where the girls' line crossed ours we tripped. . . .

Outside in the perfect snow we beat
our angel's wings. And I saw you walking
that night, Miss Devoe, with what's
his name, and I was late, I knew
even then, like the weight of the whistle. It's far
and I give it back now, that straightened world.

Mr. Wicker, I'm sorry—and all of you.

Schooling, Then and Now

Sure, I'd do it over
under a green sky going wholly blue
as I remember it, and with my bursting self
just coming up for air, it seemed, now and then,
like one of the smaller fishes, the blow-
fish whose belly relentless we tickled
until it blew up on its backside like a bubble
and blew apart too like a balloon popping,
and its tail fit for soup that's all.

Sure, I'd be better now, I'm sure of it,
and wouldn't carry still the small shames—those that
made the examples: Remember the cats
curiosity killed? The orange butterfly almost
buttery in the spring riding up into
one fist's worth of dirt not meant to. . . ?
The ducklings sick and better off . . .
The friend who didn't come back on Monday
from fishing and said to be just as well . . .

Yes, I'd do it right, or better, now that
I've been to N. Professor St. (in Oberlin, where)
and made arrangements: If I die there,
my body's to be moved before anything.
I've a lowly existence elsewhere, always looking up to
the student with my face. S.Q.,
who used to say, "Tickle my wig" to mean
different things, actually perished
in a country dump, and a truckload that backed up

and didn't care and didn't notice.

Learning, Any Time

We were singing one day about justice
and a piece of iron fell somewhere
down the street—at least I think
it was justice: it was iron all right.

One time we were early for the rainbow. Lightning
waited, crawling for a place to go.
It would decide in a minute, and then
forget in the gray cloud and maybe stay home.

It is hard to learn that zigzag before
it happens, and not much use after
it's gone—you hold your head still and wonder
about the world: you can't catch it,
    no matter how far or wide or hard.

Strange how things in the world go together
even when you don't try, how music
permeates metal, how a burden you carry
takes on a color or leads to a dream
    you are going to have when the burden is gone.

Learning, they call it, this anticipated
lightning, this thinking around an event
and bringing it right. It is hard to tell
if the connection is yours, or the world's—
    it all comes together and you say, "I know."

But the biggest things and the smallest keep right on.
What's the difference if you understand?—
the heavy will keep on being heavy, and the things
that will get you will get you just the same.

Turning on a Lamp

OK, I've got to hurry now—
we had a test for a great tenor or soprano:
their voices cracked glass . . . once.
In every little Russian town
boys like my father would remember
the man who lay under a board of nails
over which the horses ran . . . once.
In a certain American city where we were young
we had a test for cockroaches:
Turn on the light. They passed the test.
Into the country, we had a test for a tree:
Would it attract lightning?
It did, and a seam in it smoked
for two days and then it failed a test
for disease. But then *it* had a test for the ax.

Here's my own thirteen-year-old on tests:
"If you answer a question, you will be wrong,
but if you don't answer then the answer
you would have given would have been right."

I love it. My boy of twenty
studies and passes—left school, says now
one must be tough but not mean.
I can't think up the test question
for which that is the answer, though surely
it is right. You see the problem
of glory and signs of life. You see now
the way wrong schooling works—
turning on a lamp to study the dark.

Then they give you a time limit. Did I make it?

Testing, Testing, Not Being Lost

Wherever you are you hear it, a hum
other sounds can't quell, a thread you
can follow the way a bloodhound follows
a trail, never lost, because what was there
is there.

Sometimes you wander for days, try
to hear louder that silence that waits
behind other voices; but always there's something
like snow whispering the Gypsy message
into your ear . . .

—And you're off, questing again, hearing
too well to be lost: there is a place
in the world you own by failing to own
where you are, that you always know you can find
any time.

Wherever You Are

[1]

A thin silver whistle
and the dog can hear it, but it's late
for Prince and the puppy that got loose.
Prince had a bed behind the store
and a friend at the butcher. Got himself
hit by a car in the stomach
and came within a gloved hand of the end
but faced up to the chloroform
with a dogged friendliness that signalled health
and sapped him for another week.
He was my father's, and knew things.
The way a dog's ears will stand up,—
that's the way Prince caught on and stood up.

[2]

He had this thought and that thought,
I'm sure of it. Another dog was a summer
many years later, and I could ask him
to find my son in the woods. Dogs who saved
whole families in fires, who walked home
for hundreds of miles, who died within
a week or two of their owners—
they could hear the place where their absence
reshaped the air, that grave sound.

I have heard a few things before
they were said. It's nothing like the giraffe,
who says nothing, or the dolphin, who hears
it all: it's an open ear

ready for the slightest squeeze of air:
a cough of vocal muscles tensing,
a rubbing in the throat, the muscular.
It's the mutt in me, that's all.

To be "man's best friend" might be
to listen so well it needn't be said.
To hear up high, to know the thing that isn't

yet. Then what must it mean
to be death's best friend . . . ?

Dear Marvin,

I merge with your message "Wherever
You Are." I learn what it is like to
have soft ears that compose whatever comes
into a symphony, to hear as a silver
sound the whole imminent world.
You wake up my instinct for puppyhood
and bring that summer bubble around me:
forgiveness everywhere, a yearning, a grace
coming out of awkwardness to capture
us, a touch from the beginning of things.

These beings that call each other "Prince"
or "Queenie" or "Duke," they can fetch
history along with reminders, nothing
ever quite ending—even a rose
twining out a tapering faintness toward other
seasons; and all things coming are announced
by a computer chip of sense that embodies
where they are from and how long on the way.

For awhile, reading your lines, I ran
on your trail so well I could never be lost.
And sometimes when you turned I was already
there, your very best friend

—BILL.

About Our Series

And you, Bill, remind me that poetry is something that isn't poetry, what non-poets mean when they say, "That's poetry."

The world's a wheel, alright, a little knowing and presence and a long build-up that sends up our long ideas of what is natural, while we turn through "excess" that is only being, trees that are only treeful awaiting our seeing, and a silence around to receive whatever's . . . I was going to say "good."

One man's lack of feeling is another man's edge of night. One woman's dried leaf is another's tablet. And still the official question seems to be, "What's pretty?" I want to say, "Pretty is as pretty does," and offer instead, "What's ugly?" I think the brain is superior to any idea! (No such thing as interruption.)

One of your mountains has erupted—more than Pompeii! For some, salvation was living elsewhere. I try to be there from here by looking hard at the pictures, the tiny fallen firs the newspaper means to stand for trees, the wash of ink that covers seven inches of ash, the aerial cast of the camera that looks at the mud-floods for what is underneath, the new word "lava-dam" that holds up its worst promise. And I know this distance is crucial, that none know the particulars of others, each fleeing the lava in his own way, the lucky-for-now ones choosing or choosing not to make up a life of the spirit—each person's choice, the place we can know. So I'll give you this local beginning of mine, for we've no mountain here:

The Iowa River

To be as much of oneself as possible.

To accept (& complete), rather than revise.

To fill the form (organic, human) when it appears.

A passion for philosophy, for following a path,
  for crossing a river, walking an embankment,
  for circling the whole, for bridging the river.

The wish to return, which is to go on living in what was
  and also is still—but for backward notions of time and
  the trendy, love of the crane and wrecker.

To live in. To move toward silence. To go along
  in such a way that one cannot be missed.

To be selfless. To be the time it took to be,
  nor any moment.

To be the indistinct many. Always to be
  accorded a place. Limitless goal for a wish.

Accepting What Comes

In a mirror so deep it's forever I see
that river come back, turning the whole world
around. Friends, it became like the Yukon
when I said, "Go away and leave me alone"—

But it gave me something to give you, here,
in my hand: this page. I write on it
what I find out there in any country. Please promise
to read it so well it will happen again—

Those turns, those dark little trees at the end
of the road, and the twang when the river appears,
a sudden long curve braced against
a horizon too grand for the eye to believe.

Friends, I tell you it's gold, it is better
than gold, if you learn to accept what you find.

Air Wisconsin

The day that Mt. St. Helens
gave your air a twist, seeding it,
marbling it, making it mildly ex-
plosive from your Canada to your
Salem, there came, to our Wisconsin,
a roving, dazzling rainfall
held by eighty-mile vertical winds
which simply blew a plane out of the air.

Think of those confident wings,
getting more of what they thought they wanted.
I saw them carry the pilot on a board
through mud and soybeans—
it was a film I saw in my own home
of the severed wings, the rescue
of the wounded by tractor,
the clean sheets on the black and blue

field. They were going to Nebraska's
Lincoln, when they fell into a machine
that cuts a fuselage open like a can—
the Patrol calls it the Jaws of Life.
All in little figures on a screen—
boys in mud to their ankles held up
pristine plastic bags of plasma
and a kneeling man asked, "Where does

it hurt?" And then, in recognition,
"You don't know?" I didn't.
Then the film of the volcano came on
and I could see how much the mountain
was covered by smoke—the plume,
they called it, bringing to mind
the old question from childhood:
Which weighs more: a ton of feathers
or a ton of coal? You have ten seconds.

Living Far Enough Away

"it was a film I saw in my own home
of the severed wings"

At the shop in my brain where everything happens—at the
edge, or caught in the wind—people scream,   [grunsel
and I don't want to know how they die.

Where murders are canceled, at the shop in my brain that forges
my deeds, a terrible flash almost reaches out
for the help of my hands—but then is contained.

And a storm in the mountains—only soft clouds to you—
is killing: avalanche, the vise of cold, a wrenching
death, too near—I turn away.

If you lived there, buffeted, right where everything happened,
you would be sorry. And sometimes I think nothing is far
enough, and there are things that shouldn't happen at all.

But maybe they do.

At the Writing Conference

The bindweed I put on our table
the last time, Bill, drank up slowly
its air-tailored, light-lined
soft goblet of self, all the while
we were getting ideas from you and
us and him and them, and coffee
in paper cups stood there like portions
of winter and all around the room
warming up to just being.

The bindweed was closing.
It lay on its heaviest part

as if on a kernel of density
unimaginable in an open flower
so held by its silken shape, its
parachute, its being as it was.
I put it on our table—this goblet,
parachute, this flower pulling together
its dresses—and there inside an hour
it took on weight, which once was light
and nipped the air with impunity.

Sometimes we happen where the bindweed
closes up and prying fails
and scissors find no life anywhere.
Where words go into the past
and we can't help it or each other.
But sometimes we happen where the bindweed
is open, weightless; where, heedless,
it becomes something—almost leaving
its ground, twining, gathering.

Trouble is always asking.
Flowers are always answering.

More than Words Can Tell

. . . words go into the past
and we can't help it or each other

Don't ask, "Are you afraid?"—
everyone is afraid. Ask, "Where
can we find to run?" Then maybe a mountain
moves, and their instant faces freeze
as the mountain falls toward the past:—a lake
touches the sun; in a long slow wave
millions of people pour; a road
opens, for miles into a forest
and over a plain. . . . All of this floods
their faces in that one great look that comes.

Conscious Dog

"Where to run?" I have thought such a thought
so late at night it seemed I could enter
a spot inside my right shoulder
that has hurt off and on for ten years,
or could go from one side of the brain to the other
(in one, numbers are notes; in the other,
notes are numbers). I think differently
on the far side of midnight, and like to remember
the late night Long John show from New York
talking ESP, clairvoyance, and the barber
who went to Venus: claims to sleep by
but then to wake to knowing all claims
right and wrong are out there to be received,
wavelengths bowing to each isolate star,
voices that said yes, that said no, then the planets
reflecting—so that our own words return to us
and we think because they come from elsewhere,
they are right. They are what pours,
what swallows, touches, freezes and floods.
They are what gives us the idea
we are the one part that hurts or is happy.
The messages come in as I doze off, radio on,
and they are always clear
about who and what and when and why. Then I feel
that the one question neither words nor numbers
are fit to, the one which will keep us in business,
the one to which God bows and theories of matter
are secondary to, is that old one: Where?
If the universe is expanding, what is it
that is not expanding? We sleep to go there.

Reading at American University

Start with a doorbuster, how to get in from
LaGuardia, say, or whether your transfer will
work on the underground, real directions.
Wherever you are, some little sound comes
and you answer, a tap on the waterpipe, a faint
rub on the wall. You listen. The Count of
Monte Cristo had to live like this for years.
When he came out he was a symphony
of revenge. For you it's easy. You never
owned a kingdom. You never even
expected anyone to tap back a message.
Now everyone pays attention; they notice.
"Why don't you look out where you're going!" they yell.
And you're grateful: you exist. And you know how
to get in from LaGuardia—there's a bus. And though
your transfer won't work on the underground, you know
other ways. You tap carefully on the pipe:
"I'm here, I'm here." Such a beautiful sound.

Who's In Charge Here?

I saw him hanging from the cab window,
bent at the waist, and I braked alongside.
He had just jackknifed onto the shoulder
and he was drunk and he was tired and he

was late to Chicago with perishables.
Someone stopped and brought out a thermos
of coffee. He didn't mind. It didn't
change a thing. He took in his awkward arms

the whole grill of that worthy mammoth
and kissed it and said, "I take good care
of her and she takes care of me,"
and put his mouth to it and pushed his chest to it

like a prisoner against his bars
but mostly like a trucker on a timetable
in a rig that could mostly have its way
with any thinking man with a tuft of good sense.

I didn't say, "Look out where you're going."
He would. He shook my hand hard, showing me.
Then he became his truck again, and I my car
to cross a river—that's where the highway was going.

What to Say

Sometimes you hear it from strangers, talkers
waiting in line. They know the winters
in Finland, or how the happy hours in Hawaii
bring out stories of alcohol that makes
a relaxed baby of someone, and they
survive in the surf or the snow. "God
looks after them." Such times, you want to be firm:
"No." There are names you could tell, wrecks
you tried to gather up. Some of those names
you could float from a balcony. Some drop,
some stick in your throat. One of them
you never say, for fear it might lift
all it touches—and it shouldn't. You keep it
locked up: while that name was in it, the world
glowed. But an engine was running. Whatever
you touch now means that one other time,
that ignites. Flame follows flame, and the world
is a word on fire that you have to hold.

All else is evasion: you turn aside and
whisper, but steam hisses from the surf, or the snow.
You don't want to say anything. You look
at the stranger in line and then look away.
A name tugs at your hand: you say, "No."

Zero

Flame followed flame. The volunteers
had a game, a tournament of hooks and ladders
and hoses that could break a leg.
When aluminum came in, a man could sit
on the top of a ladder and be
he would have to climb. And there was
thrown upward to a scaffolding. With wooden ladders,
screeching of pumper trucks
and hook-ups and fierce streams to fill
a target-topped bucket.
When I think of my father's coats,
I always remember a jacket I never saw:
the one that caught on fire
at the edge of a field (and he had to get out
of it fast and throw it in).
Most of the fires were north of the tracks—
poor town. Oh but my father ran
at the siren, and the barber and the radio
repairman ran, and the truck barely slowed
to catch them. We went too, on running boards
of anybody's car behind them.
It was a chase—we caught a form of water,
spreading out, we caught grief in blankets
and gutted houses—the thrill we felt to be called
faded, though I took pictures
for the paper, inked heavily to show
the black aftermath, the whole zero.

Before It Burned Over

A Sioux Grass Chant

World carpet, robe, every leaf
to look at, brought forth by
buffalo, green places maker, our
own ocean, mother of bodies and
receiver of them, arriving long ago
beginning from wind, seeker
like water of whatever touches
back, aware of stars even after
daylight or blind under snow, far
blanket, bed when we sleep, or in
that long sleep when we become
waving selves, brothers, sisters,
marching together all over the world.

What the Czar Said to the Grass

—Serious things. Deep things. A growing
awareness also carried on
by many little people each standing in one place
in an orchard; also, in town,
by coopers, carpenters, glovers and smiths,
by a potter, a plumber, a tinker,
a letterman—in another language, you understand.

I always go back there. Then there is no wind,
no green places—nor stars, nor sound.
I see people who had their pictures taken.
They stuck their chins out,
people who had never seen a boat
who brooded until they burned to cross.
An old world brought to the new:

How could it have been otherwise?
What did they have? —Their names. Probably,
that's why. Those names went up on
diplomas, trophies, granite cornerstones,
but also up on helmets and taped onto
fatigue jackets in boot camp. They would.
They would burn the grass in many places

to get the Czar and the Bolsheviks both
to lie down with them.

Just Some Names

If it's just "the weather" or "the season," they
move indoors or out or put on mittens,
but if it's "The Czar" or some other kind
of name, like revolution or lack of
it, they have a language of anger;

And by combining blame with reason
they become a people: they form societies
and govern and go to war. Some of them
stay cool, study, and shake their heads;
but others parade and counter-parade.

If it's going to be reason, if
the anger has words that mean more than
just sounds, there must be a still place
in the sky, where names can snuggle together
and live like the weather: Snow-Czar, Fyodor,
Bell, Bill, Fidel, Ronnie.

"Words that Mean More
than Just Sounds"

One of my favorites is,
"She had to sell the tires to buy the gas."

In dirt-floor-only places in Mexico,
a ga-ga tourist was told, "You can't sell the scenery."

My father from my mother was
"as different as chalk from cheese."

Someone was "touched."
Another was "peculiar." Hence,

I know the meaning in, "The rain
is too heavy a whistle for the certainty of charity."

I can answer, "Where was it they went to do,
the young engaged off on their own at last?"

Or if asked, "Wasn't the water a lubricant
on your way to the sea of sorrows?" I can say.

But best may be this, and all like it
(this one's a Polish grandmother's):

"Ah skah, snella pella,
sinka pinka, hossa possa,

snella pella poof!
Goggledy, feggledy, quakoose!"

On a lined index card, my son prints NORMAL
and underneath, "Nothing special happening."

Nothing Special

Someone was by the glass in the door. It was late.
I wasn't at home. What happened was this:
they tried. And their picture, or a mask—
the rays told all. Those rays always came.
So I tried to be kind, but I knew. And when
they found they were guilty, they looked at the scanner
again, and the rays went off the scale at them.

Now in the night a wind comes, or trucks
are running somewhere, their lights making
long arcs in mist—whatever: it is dark
where we are. And here comes the fire of knowing
until we doze off again. That all these events
happened, that the track through the scanner
cleared often, and recorded—I am sorry to throw
all that away. Somewhere it still happened,
even after we changed, I am going to believe,
though the world won't mean so much to us
any more. It's a deep loss. I let the trucks
have all the rest of the night, and I keep a soft little
engine beating, or just wings and a dim reflection
that won't make anything happen, but is here, still here.

That all those events happened,
that we could never throw all that away—
somewhere it still happened, even after
we changed. I am going to believe, though,
that world won't mean anything to us
any more. I let the trucks have the night,
but keep a dim reflection from what happened:
somewhere it still happened. But that world
won't mean anything to us any more,
I am going to believe.

Then

Those light shows on the bedroom walls—
they were wonderful to go to sleep by,
a child waiting for his parents and maybe
in the morning there'd be a toy when I woke.

Very little I wanted, my father's 5 & 10
a kind of museum that satisfied me.
Reading the ouija board with my sister,
the message was always, "Go to sleep, Marvin."

Sometimes Jessie Q. sat for me, whose house
had burned so now she lived in a roofed basement.
She gave me clumps of coins joined by fire,
and I could read in them the value of loss.

I would lie in bed and spread the light
with my fingers, and then there might be animals
or odd shapes to see there, cars passing—
I could count the trees by flickerings—

and then the shapes that slid the walls
became a calligraphy, and the signs a language
and the language a sound, and then the dark
proceeded and I did not interrupt it.

It Still Happens Now

You make me walk my town, its terrible
streets that peel day after day for years
and fall into the sky, till I'm drowned
in time. Even if I shut my eyes the lilacs
come their tide, and Pauline's old house
honks by in a long, low, dying moan
as I fade for my life, wild for this safety
of now, far from the thousand hurts—
those friends moving there still,
fresh, open faces, long bodies leaning
after my last goodby, when war came, and
we left all that seething, and put the lid on.

Crooked Water Ways

We ran down the street to get away from . . . There
was Brooklyn Dock (not a shipyard, our own tire-lined
wharf for clammers, weekenders' outboards, inboards
weighted for speed and local fame
and a few spiffy skiffs or something visiting, such as
one of those sleek sailers made iceboats in winter).

So we took what we found, prow to the wind, angling
the whitecaps, lying in the bottom when cruisers, heedless,
churned so close their wakes swamped us,—
up again up again (afloat!) to row and bail.
(We always involved a tin can and a board.)

These weren't our boats, exactly. They belonged.
We thought our way: there were the boats,
there was water, and there was time. Two of three
belonged to anyone who used them. We were young.
Being two-thirds right seemed like quite a lot to be.

Now I don't say we were thieves, or we weren't.
Mr. Johnson, the Bank Manager, walked with a stoop
the months his Kenny manned a machine gun in Korea.
Sandbags and dead corporals were the news then.
Kenny came home by boat but something had been taken.
He had had to go to hell to get permission.

Key of C—an Interlude for Marvin

Sometime nothing has happened. We are home
at the beginning of summer. Somebody begins
to breathe chords on a harmonica.
"Why don't we tell how our lives will be?"
Sarah says—"I'll start: when I finish
college I'll move East and work in
a bank. In a robbery there a stray bullet
will kill me." Tom quits playing the harmonica:
"I'll work in Dad's drugstore. My wife and child
will die in a fire when the child is three."
He goes on breathing slow notes. Mary
leans back in the porch swing: "I'll marry Tom
and oh I'll hold the little one so close."
"I see exactly," Steve says: "After The War
I'll come back here and you'll all be gone. I don't
want to tell the rest." They turn to me:
"I'll live carefully, and a long time.
Years from now when I'm writing to a friend
I'll tell him what we said today
and how it all came true." —And, oh Marvin,
even this part I'm telling you.

The Years 1950–54

There's always some water in the grass next to the tracks.
There's always a trumpeter calling.
I couldn't draw and wouldn't learn.
I was good at wearing hats, but you know that.

A green canal came into town almost to Main,
dead at one end.
My father thought I should be
a psychiatrist—because it took a lot of schooling.

Classes were an interlude in between free times.
I was like a duck on land.
There will always be flounder and weakfish.
The jellyfish was our octopus; the shark, our mammoth.

The crab went sideways. Light broke our nets. We knew
the crab is always lower
than he seems: water plays tricks.
The counselor thought I should be a psychiatrist.

I was like a duck on land, or a wheel in sand.
I spotted planes at the dock
for the Air Force,
mostly unidentified except for the box-tailed Lockheed
                                             [Lightnings.
A girl from Westhampton lost her Air Force father
and the band played *Going Home*.
I wanted to fly and looked up to people.
This grown-up thing of going deeper hadn't begun.

Now I see those pinwheels in lawns vibrating in the dirt
to make the mole swerve.
If I pull them up, what's that?
The mole swerves. Have you ever seen a duck go uphill?

For an OK Writer

You make it happen—the world out there
jumps at us through windows and unfolds
what didn't happen all around outside.
Part of our gift of time wanders
those infra-red, ultra-violet scenes
acted through unlimited corridors in limbo.

And other selves crowd forward—they lift
the old neighborhood call, "We are here
waiting for you to come out to play."
These walls become nothing. Only
artificial glass ever held us inside
a room. We shatter into that palace
called outdoors. You open it. You make it happen.

Seeing that Things Happen

A mothballed fleet offshore fell out of war
and now when you see them there off the highway
their boat-forms merge with a grey industrial sky
in New Haven, Connecticut, and they look like clay
destroyers, unopposed, beautiful and happy.

In Arizona, the sand shifted and spread out,
absorbing the green at the far edges of waving
golden air, and the goldenness of the heat,
and the whites and blues of flame and sore reds,
and now it's the Painted Desert no one believes.

Even things that happened have to happen
when we're up to being amazed, undeprived, speechless;
and there's room for dedication in this
and pilgrimming, back-packing of letters, diminished
real voices lost at sea or crowned by thirst,

restated in a wind—across neutral planes.